GOOD NIGHT, NURSE

Early Emotion and Poetry of
LLOYD MATTHEW THOMPSON

STARFIELD

Starfield Press
Oklahoma City, OK

GOOD NIGHT, NURSE

Early Emotion and Poetry of
LLOYD MATTHEW THOMPSON

LIST OF POEMS BY FIRST LINE

GOOD NIGHT, NURSE

Early Emotion and Poetry of
LLOYD MATTHEW THOMPSON

This volume you now feast your eyes upon is the encompassing collection of my early experiences and emotions that found their way out of me in their process of processing, and onto a page in one way or another. The typical birth places for most of these were little yellow sticky notes. Some came out quick and whole, perfectly formed in my head. The words of others were whittled and tweaked until the sticky note was so covered with scribbles and scratches the replacement words had to be written in sideways to fit. In either case, and all in between, what resulted was always my attempt to make outward sense of my inward clutter.

Once finalized, I always neatly hand-copied them into a suede-bound volume I kept of all my work, in sequential order. Some sort of historian or archivist apparently also lives inside me.

I refer to this period of my life as "The Flailing Years." As I came out of what I'd been raised with and all I'd ever known, I followed my Heart through alleys and staircases, struggling to find my way and my self. From shifty religions and spiritual concepts to rocky relationships and family drama, I sought my truth with every breath.

The poetry in this collection is not all I've ever done, of course. I arranged this compilation in 2006, after reading through my entire black suede poetry journal and selecting the verses I felt best captured my evolution. It seemed I was entering a new age, and the same internal librarian that had previously driven me to record and preserve all my work now pushed me to "finalize" that closing chapter of my life.

And so I chose the following sixty-nine poems to represent the me I used to be, in this ritual of closure and moving on.

I had intended at that time to self-publish them in a printed volume, and make them available through my personal website of artwork and writing. That never happened.

The year is now 2012, nearly 2013. Technology has failed at changing its habits of never slowing down for even a fraction of a nanosecond, and the eBook publishing industry has now skyrocketed quicker than Mr. Armstrong (who undertook his own moving on this year) did on his way to step on our moon. As I formulate other projects and books for this brave new world, I felt it was time to finally complete the ritual begun over six years ago, and officially close that block of my life.

Whether my work is read or enjoyed is not of importance to me. The completed endeavor holds all the intention and power for me.

Also, you will find these poems are not in chronological order. As organized and structured as I've been known to be, I do not believe time flows in a linear line, and therefore the jigsaw pieces of one's life should not be a solid straight line either.

I picked the poetry that made the final cut, and placed them in a hat. The Universe then picked the arrangement. And— as with all that It touches— it randomly ordered a perfect order.

I've removed the original numeric titles, dates, and timestamps (I told you I was detailed!) from each verse, for a more integrated oneness, but these words span from approximately 1994 to 2006.

One hope I do hold for this collection is that someday somebody will see this journey of mine, and be inspired on their own journey. Perhaps one of these phrases that poured from my Heart and Mind will leap off the page and smack them on the forehead, rendering their suffering unconscious, or in the very least, give voice to their own fettered emotions and experiences.

At any rhyme or reason, I thank you deeply for taking the time to give this personal collection of mine a second glance. I may not be anything like the person you will find in these poems anymore, but they will forever be a brick in the wall of who I now am— and who I have yet to be.

Lloyd Matthew Thompson
November 2012
Oklahoma City, Oklahoma, USA

To all the ones who made me grow,
by pain or love, pull or shove —
You know just who you are.

He wept from three little words…

GOOD NIGHT, NURSE

A capture of present —
Immediate past
What you see before Thee
Will not always last
Already a mem'ry
Look past and see
The Future zip past
At immeasur'ble speed
Even Present from Past
Has already passed —
The Key to the Present
Is the Gift of the Past

— • —

And it walked in
Quickly yet
Slowly yet
Entrancing yet
Dreams

And it took out
Defenses but
Strengthened but
Rejected but
Loved

And it offered
All things or
Nothing or
Chocolate or
'Nilla

And it shattered
The hope and
The hopeless and
Excitement and
Doom

And it walked out
Quickly yet
Slowly yet
Entrancing yet
Dreams.

— • —

Manifesto!
What I've carried up these stairs
These twenty-seven years
Has come as far as I'll allow —
It's going out the window now!

Whatchoutbelow!
The sidewalk is now splattered
With insecurities ashattered.
Let that jealous puddle rot,
And avoid that mistrust spot!

Becausey'know!
The end has come at last —
This future's NOT the past!
I now bow unto the one
Who has caused this to be done...

Iletitgo!

— • —

How did you like the Weather today?
Wasn't it lovely the way that it changed?
I figured the twister had had all its fun
But of course it was waiting
'Till my Cellar had run

Out of its stock and
Out of its hold
Out of its mind
Unlike we were told

You have all the power
You feel it inside
But the language of body
Causes "V"ision to hide
Shadows for hoodies
Miscontact for hi
Speak up! and
Look up!
For yours is the Sky!

What if the Pattern was somehow the same?
Would you become mute to discover their name
Was spelled out in Riddles exactly like yours?
Painted and sculpted in
Images yours?

Identity blurred, focus
Classified for
Only the ones with their Box in the rain
The ones with their Crayon outside of the page
Living and Breathing
Among the Insane

Aren't you flipping those channels too fast?
The frequency's higher'n that knob there can go.
Put on your Shoes and get ready to go
Cut off the power and taste of this Snow
Accept all this yes and replace all this no
This place is becoming abandoned soon, no?

This is the Here and
This is the Now
Are you sure that that Planet
Can fit into that Pocket?
Account for the Moon and
Make space for the Rocket.

What does that gong in the Distance foretell?
What is that chanting b'weaving a spell?
Why is your Heart-ache b'thumping to hell?
Is it the Passion? Is that what just fell?
Your shadow no longer is looking so well.

Buy it and
Try it and
See if it's true.
What could you lose
But a Minute or two?

— • —

Not so timid as before.
Older,
Colder,
More mature.
Strength inside the big and brown.
Bolder,
Colder,
Unheld down.

— • —

Caught when least expected,
The virus woke and took control.
Toxication, medication —
Harmless, adaptation.

A blade of grass was all,
To bring the mighty to its knees!
Captivated, rapture-ated,
Focus concentrated.

The level was so high,
It drowned inside the frost, but then
Thawed out into a work of art,
To find the key to heart…

— • —

Do thoughts of what you said
Swim around inside your head?
Can you even sleep at all,
Or do you not even recall
The lies and twisted schemes
You told and did to get your dreams?
At the cost of someone's life,
You tried to turn around your strife
But only made the matter worse,
For now you have the triple Curse
With restless sleep and nightmare dreams,
Of causing pain and silent screams.
You got your old ways back again,
But are you happy with a grin?
If all you said of him was true,
Then I don't see how it would do.
That made of love turned out of lust,
Leftovers from the previous.
You HAD to have known it from the start
And conned your way, for bills and heart.
And did you think about the little one?
Our bond was strong— is she undone?
They knew me better than you realized—
The truth can't hide from children's eyes.
I'll be honest, as I must do.
I miss them more than I miss you.

My path moves on...

— • —

The wall of the post office
Crumbled today
The posters were nailed
But too many to stay
MISSING! they screamed
Have you seen me?
Hundreds,
Nay, thousands,
Nay, millions away
Belongings remain
But bodies go play
POOF
All at once
Twinkled away…

(I Cor. 15:52)

— • —

And beat plays on...
And on burns the sun...
And sunburns some more...
And more is exposed...
And exposed is the Soul...
And Soul...

Is...

Beat...

And beat plays on....

Hey! Is that a light up ahead?

— • —

Every person she meets
She inevitably fucks,
I'd like to find out
Who made *her* Queen of Lucks.

Things get to be swell
Then turn right into hell —
Until I see reason…
Perception, Reaction, New Season!

— • —

I am your hero
Your Grand Escape
The Ticket
The OneWay
I am living Tape.

But.

I am the wrapper
Feet on the ground
It won't be
Long until
You are not around.

So.

I am the Shadow
You cannot rape
The hermit
'Till one day
I get to escape…

— • —

Another is no more
One that was here
And held so dear
And one all did adore
Has carried on, you see—
Not simply ceased to be!

— • —

SHE'S EITHER WITH ME
OR SHE'S NOT—
ALL OTHER THOUGHTS
CAN FUCKING ROT!
JUST SET HER FREE
AND LET HER BE—
ENCOURAGING
IN LOVE WITH ME!

— • —

Bottlecaps
Once three-dimensional
Confining alcoholic beverages
In their twelve ounce
Fragile prisons
Now lay untouchable
Immovable
With but one dimension left
Compressed into an altered state
Reality is Radial.

— • —

The Future of the Past
Is now made known to me at last
It finally dropped its natural mask
And in its nature I now ask
How can you shut it off like so?
What happened to our lantern glow?
Now was it ever real at all?
Or for a fourth now did I fall?
Sit in the Sun and soak it in!
And let the Red be read again.

— • —

Yellow grass
Reminds me that
Winter
Is still here.

I miss Green,
Much better, Red
Why was
Black not there?

Blue escapes,
Replaced by Grey
Shade of
Deeper Sad.

Faded White
Sun-dried to Taste
Where has
That Color gone?

— • —

Where have you been? O Where have you been?
I whispered inside, and just wondered when
What I knew that first time would come 'round again,
Sooner than dreamed, 'twas returned to me then
Where have you been? O Where have you been?

— • —

Sun that burns and moon that glows,
Point to me what I should know…
Whisper wind and babble brook,
Tell me where I am to look…
Destiny is truly mine,
I want to be where I can shine…

— • —

The Hinder is the Holding
The Block is called Remorse
The snatching of the Vapor
Unwandering of Course

Entrusting all the Being
Unto Another Life
Proves to be an Undertow
Ungrounding and the Eyes

Pour out their Corners when the
Dreams forget the Dawn
Is not Sunset yet even
Beginning is now gone

The Orbit of the Planets
Reaching far into the Night
Find Gravity is nothing
To be Dabbl'd even light

The glass upon the Hour
Radiates a crimson Glow
The One who made the Lantern
Gently beckons and I know

The Retrograde's Direct and
The Fork now has a Sign
The Fingers at the Keyboard
Strike up a Tune Divine

— • —

But so many turn their eyes,
Hide their tears and chant the lies
"Not my problem, not my problem!"
But what if the next were them,
And there was not an outstretched Hand —
Compassion famine in this Land!
But that that's entered under Heaven
Returns to One — at times by Seven.

— • —

The cramping of the hand...
The tingling of the leg...
The sipping of the coffee...
The numbing of the cold...
The churning of the mind...
The bubbling of the mem'ry...
The storming of the stereo...
The unlocking of the Soul.

The ice comes down and tickles my window!
Is it the same as rain?
I did not realize I was starving
Until I woke again.

— • —

The blood no longer flows
Through your heart
You've sealed and closed
Your every part
To hold the pain you chose
You must start
To break the wall that grows —
Do your part.

— • —

Another year gone
You say
Another year gone
And lay
Your head down inside
Your grave
And lift up your voice
And pray
Please take all this pain
Away
Let me live life one
More day

— • —

I look up towards the light
And wait for guidance.
Others around me move along
While I am not allowed
Until I receive the signal
That it is time.
When it comes, I feel the rush.
Done is the wait
I take my foot off the brake
And
Accelerate.

— • —

Int'resting to know
Soon as I let go
Words and Images aflow
Floodgates open to bestow —
Other Minds I then a-sow!

— • —

The same way I stayed with you is
The same way I now stay apart and
The same way I loved you so is
The same way it tears out my heart…

— • —

The sun sets down and once again
I'm here alone without a friend
The rain that falls outside tonight
Successfully demonstrates the mood of this plight
Perfection is locked in and out of a cage
The Universe's games tease and taunt rage
Helpless I lay here— when will it end?
How many more thorns in my side will you send?

— • —

Always
You say
The words are useless
What's the use?
Until later you see
And amazement descends
And brings you back
To where you've been.
Always.

— • —

Faltering on
A balance beam
Edge of a cliff
About to scream
And wondering
The Sun it seems
Has turned to Green
The Satellite
Reflects to me
A quarter sheen
A quota three
More Blue than Green
About to scream
But looking Down
I see the Stream
That brings a Leaf
Bears also Grief—
Pain and Relief
And the Sun it seems
Burns on all three
How can that be when
There's more to Me
Than this?

— • —

Illusion of wholeness,
Completely deceived
A hardened clay pot
With hammer in hand
Pounding the nails
With smile so sweet
In your hands and feet.
'Till eyeball meets eyeball
Realization descends
And guilt overwhelms.
What have I done?
Now You have the hammer,
You swing it at me
Smashing this vessel,
The redemption of me.

— • —

Chapter, Verse,
Unneeded first.
Read It through,
And that will do!

Despite the Desire,
There's more to this Fire.
A Strength from the Sun,
Independent, each One.

— • —

I breathe in.
I muddle.
I exhale.
Light.

— • —

This place is called Harmony
This place is called Rest
Regrounding, Rebalance
The cheat to the Test

Here Ashes are breathing
Here Ashes respect
The Fear and the Suff'ring
Here have no effect

Again All are one where
Again All are free
Behind or below or
Above, only Me.

— • —

And we made our decisions
What was in store
We knew full well—
Bruises, and more.

And we made our decisions
For better or worse—
But a balance is needed
To walk down this course.

And we made our decisions
For we are complete—
Whatever is coming,
We lay at His feet...

And we made our decisions
And
We
Will
Be.

— • —

Good morning, Everything!
What the heaven shall we sing?
Something like let Freedom ring?
Let Popcorn pop in the machine?
Take a breath and hear the ding —
Something's cooking in the Wing!
Father time perhaps fleeing,
Sight and touch let go, shedding
The Light abroad the deciding,
That Golden-Azul sparkling,
Soaring high so dizzying
Yet grounded so interesting,
Contradiction existing,
Heat and Chill reCycling,
Both unseparate becoming…
All that matters?
Not a thing.

— • —

Look them in the eyes,
And see through the disguise.
There is their own demise—
A bed of motherfucking lies.

— • —

This is me
All I see
Is smashing,
Crashing,
Individuality

— • —

The Light's a'hand,
The Light's afoot,
The Light's ahead,
Is what She said!

— • —

Where I was weak
and was selfish
and viewing the world through the incorrect lens,
you pushed me
and forced me
and opened my eyes.
You strengthened my strength,
and weakened my weakness.

Where I was tired and cold,
you refreshed and rejuvenated,
warmed and breathed life.

Where I was absorbed and alive,
you turned on a light,
killed off the shadow,
and replanted my roots.

If you had not come,
where,
how,
what would I be?
Still focused on me,
but not upon Me.
Still chasing a notion,
reality-blind.
In three different ways,
you helped to transform —
a major step necessary
for the next step so necessary.

You may not even know that this happened.
You may not realize
what you've done.
But that's how it works,
these fated Designs,
no sight of the Picture
in the midst of the Scheme.
Big and Grand both do no good Here.

What happened just happened,
just what happened was all
that was meant to just happen,
no more and no less.
From beginning to end,
or rather how they just be,
the Purpose was there
on either half
of the moon.

So thank you for all,
for playing along,
for doing what you were put here to do —
a piece of my life
is complete after all!

From the bottom of my Heart,
from my very Core:
thank you, I thank you…
What a Treasure you are!

— • —

I belong to no one
None belong to me
And if that's ever fashioned
Someone slap sense into me!

— • —

The current pain is always worse
Than all the ones before.
Rage caged inside, about to burst —
How can I take much more?

Can hand in hand walk love and lies?
Trust and forgiveness bought?
No matter how it's justified,
It grows decay and rot.

Addiction or fate meant to be?
Familiar or the One?
Whichever way you choose to see,
Death's work here is now done.

— • —

This was a step
A step closer There
A step farther Here
An inspiration
Brewing
Boiling
Perculating deep
InvisibleJava
In InvisibleSoul
About to spill
And Stain
The Streets
I walk.

Are you ready?
Am I ready?
Time is what's needed
Space more than abounds
It's time to Unveil
Make space for the Soul

A taste of my place makes me hungry for more.
Whether I'll shine or go down in flames remains to be seen,
but the frostbite of Winter pushed me to see...

Alone I am Me.
Just as should be.

nowfuckalltimidityandwatchoutcommunity!!!

— • —

Well THAT'S a fine
How-do-you-do —
Fuck you, too!

I understand but
Don't accept
My expectations were not kept

Well THAT'S just fine
I-don't-need-you —
Fuck, I do.

— • —

Permanent Impermanence —
Where then is my Residence?
Within a Book
Or Shutter-box?
Scratching out in paint or pen?

These pages are encaptivating,
Capture-click intoxicating,
Toxic Love is liberating —

If this is Life, then what is that?
Nothing to do with me?
Great Deceive —
Or was that we?
Turn back the Clock and we'll just see.

Turn back the Clock and we'll just be.

— • —

I stood at the crossroads last night
The one where the sign read
Throw in the towel or
Move on ahead
But my friends Hesitation
Indecision and Doubt
Had somewhere abandoned me
During the four
So the number stays three.

— • —

Alone with the spiritual
Troubled in spirit you'll
Soon come to realize
Which are my real eyes

— • —

I'm laying on the floor
Some obscured and some exposed
Vivid colors telling more
Than I'd ever know with my mind closed

— • —

Confusion and frustration
Unfortunately reside
In this fucking fucked up
Fleshy hide
It hurts the one I love
The Most
Please know that I'm an
Unwilling host
I want to do what's right
Each day,
But what that is
Who has the right to say?

— • —

If you still don't know why
I always cry
Then I don't know if I
Have any choice but goodbye…

— • —

It burns! It burns!
Will the Foolish never learn?
Like the butter, Mind is churned
Circle 'round, eternal turn
Unenlightened constant yearn
Forever patience is to Earn.

— • —

I don't think I know what love is,
I don't think I've ever known.
And if true love's to me been shown,
It hides from me, unknown.

— • —

He is fully aware,
But does not care.
He thinks he does not need
To crash and bleed
The water of the soul
And once again
Be made whole.

— • —

Oh Mighty One who broke my chains
My Father who washed away my stains
By giving Your Son, my brother and friend
I praise You, My God, and will 'til the end
I thank You for saving my life from the flood
And wiping my eyes of that mire and mud
That blinded my sight and muddled my mind
And kept hiding from me what I wanted to find.

— • —

Alas!
Autumn is closing,
Winter draws near,
The end of the age is upon us,
I fear.
The clock has been ticking
And what have we done?
None have made ready,
Not even one...
The tears of the angel
Flying midair
Shower upon us,
Ignored, do we care?
What happens next?
Twinkle and flash.
Who has been left?
The moment has passed...

— • —

In the silence of his solitude, he cried
Tears ran deep as the shudders came
He wept from sadness
He wept from regret
He wept from gratefulness
He wept from three little words

Good Night Nurse

— • —

What is Reality?
Overturning tables,
Breathing fairy fables—
Much too comforty.
Much to comefortea.

Rapping tapping at the door?
The F that means afraid,
But manhandLed by the L—
The L that is my name.
The L that is your name.

What?
Oh never mind that.
They are only chains,
Dust will arrive—
And you'll never be able to tell.
And you'll ever be able to tell.

Why should we sleep?
Life is meant to live.
I don't know your planet
But mine is red and ready—

Now to turn this Winter off…

— • —

Her shadow before Me,
Her body above,
I dance with my Lady,
In the silence make love.

With but half of her might,
She entangles the night.
Her beams fall and infect —
Left and Right ears connect!

— • —

And you
Think I'm asleep
And I
Cannot
See

And you
Think me so blind
That I
Cannot
Find

And you
Think it is sweet
But I
Cannot
Cheat

And you
And you
And you
Think it's the past
Think it would last
Think all the lies
Will burn through the cast
Think I'll use my brain
For once really fast—
I'm through
I'm through
I'm through.

— • —

Hypocrite psychotic,
Religious and robotic…

— • —

Everything, yet nothing.
The dream banished away.
Tore up inside,
A life destroyed,
Emotion gone to stay?

— • —

I want
To stay
Here
Awake
I want
To play
But
I shake

— • —

Another Life, another Life
How can it be so near?
How can it be so far?
Within it once
Without it thrice
Blind from the glare it told.

And the Return is painting nigh.

A strand of hair
A Quarter There
I think it is a Riddle
Floating in the Middle

Another Life, another Life
Why can't I smell the Daylight?
Why can't I see the Coffee?
Shut the fridge
Toss out the toast
What good is Blinking now?

Yet the Vision breathes a sigh.

The Water below
Whispers "You know!"
The Power-hum
Taunts "Not-so-numb!"

Another Life, another Life
O when can I be a Part?
When did *this* leak in my Heart?
The shutter claps
So Frost meets Thaw
But the Blood is still the same.

But I've my Own to not let die.

Now give me one more Cry.

— • —

Ah.
But cheese is so delicious!
And sap is so sensual and sweet!
And mush may too much currently abound,
But it sure makes MY world go 'round!

— • —

The river is frozen
'Til inspiration flows in

— • —

The cobwebs on the ceiling
Every thought and every feeling
All the pain and all despair
The angel from my nightmare

Explain.

The angel from my nightmare
All the pain and all despair
Every thought and every feeling
No cobwebs on the ceiling

— • —

Swallow this Pill
To loosen the tongue
And expose to me now —
I am not so young.

— • —

My heart
It's beating way too fast
A pressure crushing
In my breast
Panic causeless
That I can see
Distress unrest
Possessing me

My heart
It's beating O so fast
O grip unwanted
Mercy lest
My foot unholds!
Sadness from where
Cometh Thee?
Recess in me!

— • —

Walk away
Now walk away—
Twilight's taken
Half the Day
Anyway.

Walk away
Just walk away—
That's the way, a
Step a day,
But I say

Walk away
Don't walk away,
Ignore this way
O Baby stay
Here today…

Walk away
Please walk away
And quit this play of
Night and Day,
This fickle Fray!

Walk away,
Walkin' away
Another Day is
On the Way
Anyway.

— • —

Solitude?
Yes.
I am alone.
No, wait —
There's One,
There's Two,
There's Three in me…
We are four.
We are one.
I am not alone.

— • —

"*Enlightening, empowering...*
5-Star information!"

THE
NATURAL
HEALER'S
GUIDE

BESTSELLING AUTHOR OF *LIGHTWORKER*
LLOYD MATTHEW THOMPSON

Look for *The Natural Healer's Guide*
Only from **Starfield Press**!

LIGHT WORKER

A CALL TO AUTHENTICITY

LLOYD MATTHEW THOMPSON

Look for *Lightworker: A Call to Authenticity*
Only from **Starfield Press**!

ENERGY
WORKER

A CALL TO EMPOWERMENT

LLOYD MATTHEW THOMPSON

Look for *Energyworker: A Call to Empowerment*
Only from **Starfield Press**!